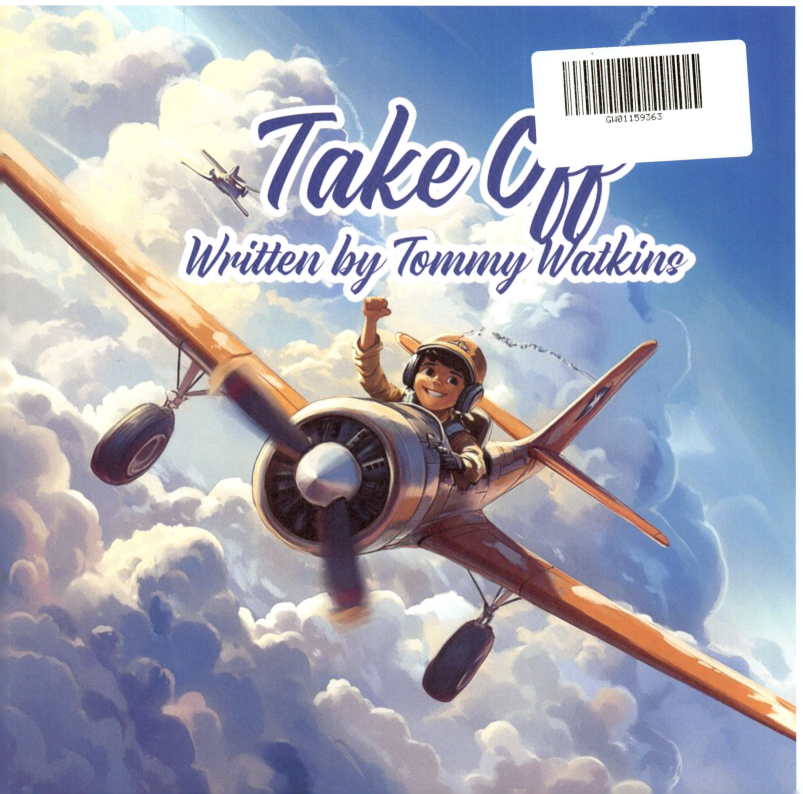

I love airplanes.
The sights and the sounds captivate me.

I graduated from school, and it's time to become a real-life pilot.

Job application after job application, soon I will get a callback.

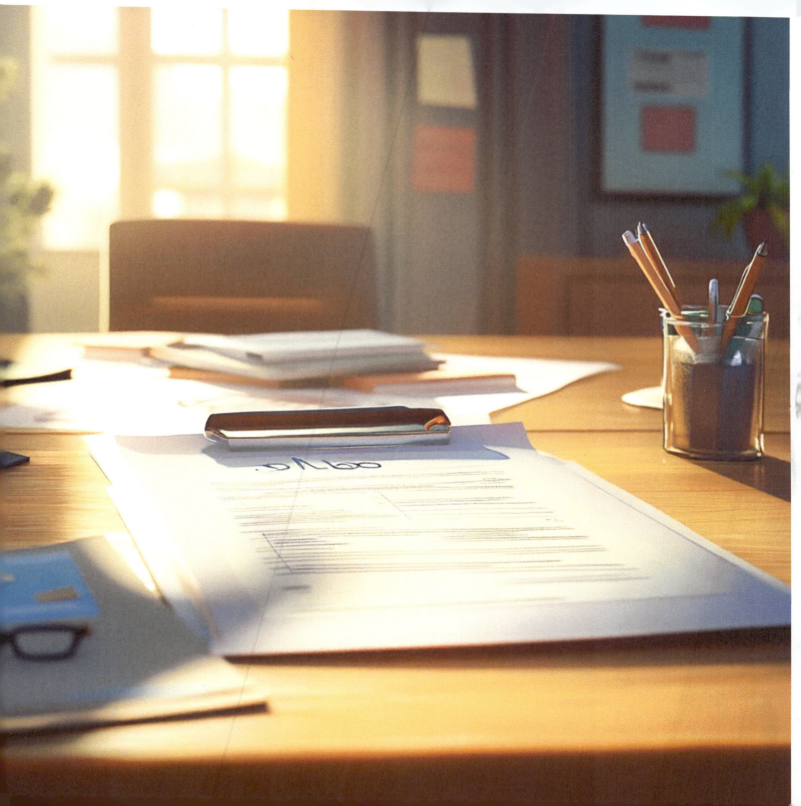

After waiting a few weeks,
I finally got a call to interview in person.

The airline tells me I am too inexperienced to be a pilot.

The bills start to pile up.
I pick up a job as a server.

The days drag on slowly as a server.
I can prove all these airlines wrong.

After my shifts at my serving job,
I work on building an airplane,
a one-seat plane
that can take me to the sky.

Finally, after one year,
my airplane is finished.
It is time to fly it in the sky.
Take Off.

The End